THE AFFORDABLE FLIGHT GUIDE:

HOW TO FIND CHEAP AIRLINE TICKETS AND SEE THE WORLD ON A BUDGET

Jen Ruiz

The Affordable Flight Guide:
How to Find Cheap Airline Tickets and See the World on a
Budget

Published by Jen on a Jet Plane
www.jenonajetplane.com/

© 2017 Jen on a Jet Plane

Cover: Abanob Design and Fi2 Design

While all attempts have been made to verify the information provided in this publication, neither the author nor the publisher assumes any responsibility for errors, omissions, or contrary interpretations of the subject matter herein.

Table of Contents

Introduction

CHAPTER ONE *Where to Find the Best Flight Deals*

1.1 Sign up for Flight Alerts
1.2 Use a Flexible Search Engine
1.3 Best Booking Practices
1.4 What's a Good Deal?

CHAPTER TWO *An Introduction to Travel Hacking*

2.1 Definition of Travel Hacking
2.2 Travel Credit Cards
2.3. Earning Miles/Points
2.4 Redeeming Your Miles

CHAPTER THREE *Flying on Budget Airlines*

3.1 Common Carriers
3.2 Avoiding Additional Fees
3.3 Buying Direct from the Airline
3.4 Pros and Cons of Budget Airlines

CHAPTER FOUR *Other Money-Saving Strategies*

4.1. Rule of Proximity and Flexibility
4.2 Mixing and Matching Airlines
4.3 Booking in a Foreign Currency
4.4 Minimizing Airport Expenses

CHAPTER FIVE *Bonus Material*

5.1 25 Free Mobile Apps Every Traveler Should Have
5.2 Best Websites for Living and Working Abroad
5.3 20 Side Hustle Ideas to Boost Your Travel Funds

About the Author

Introduction

"The journey of a thousand miles begins with one step." – Lao Tzu

For most people, the biggest deterrent to travel is the price of an airline ticket. If it only cost $50 to get to Paris, everyone would be lining up for macarons and Eiffel Tower views. Over the years, however, airlines have started offering less and charging more, taking away the things we once considered essentials, like free carry-on luggage and in-flight beverage service.

The result? Everyone wants to travel more, but few people actually do. They convince themselves they can't afford to travel and spend their lives dreaming of faraway places instead. This book is the first in a series of works meant to dispel limiting beliefs of would-be travelers, such as "traveling is expensive," "I have no one to go with" or "I can't travel because I have a real job." Over the next few chapters we will demystify the gateway to travel: cheap flights. By helping you get to your destination for less, you'll be able to travel more.

Consider this your $50 flight to Paris, or anywhere else in the world. I should know—using the tactics I'm about to reveal, I booked a trip from Miami to New Zealand for only $38. Typically, Auckland is near impossible to reach at a discounted price. Tickets run from $1,500-$2,000 roundtrip. I booked my flight for $37.70, the cost of taxes.

Your trip receipt

Jennife Ruiz Garay

TAXES AND CARRIER-IMPOSED FEES	$ 37.70
TICKET TOTAL	$ 37.70

The final route and pricing is discussed further in Section 2.4.

New Zealand isn't the only great flight deal I've found. In the past year, I have booked a $16 flight to Ecuador, $70 roundtrip flight to Aruba, $80 flight from Bangkok to Miami, $22 roundtrip flight to San Francisco and $327 roundtrip flight Argentina, among others. Some of my trips were purchased with airline miles, others were found through savvy searching strategies. My budget travel secrets have been featured by The Washington Post, ABC News, Paste Magazine and Elite Daily. Now, for the first time ever, I've compiled everything I know about finding cheap air travel into one place, your ultimate guide to affordable flights.

It doesn't matter if you're a new flyer, frequent flyer or elite status holder—the tips in this book will help you rethink how you search for deals and maximize your rewards. Once you figure out how to make flying affordable again, traveling becomes much more enticing. Any concerns you have about safety, culture shock or budgeting are secondary to getting a plane ticket in hand. So let's help you board first, and figure out the details later.

At the end of this guide, I've included several free resources, including a list of free mobile apps for the savvy traveler, side hustle ideas to help you fund your next trip and alternative work and lodging sites to help you transition to long-term travel or even living abroad.

Also, as a special bonus to my readers, I've created a page where you can find even more free content, like an introductory video, affordable flights flowchart and my ultimate carry-on checklist. Just go to my website at www.jenonajetplane.com/affordableflightguide to access all this and more, as a thank you for reading my book.

Are you ready to start saving money? Let's get started!

CHAPTER ONE
Where to Find the Best Flight Deals

"Come fly with me, let's fly, let's fly away." –
Frank Sinatra

1.1 Sign up for Flight Alerts

The quickest way to start landing great flight deals is to sign up for flight alerts. Alerts can come through a mailing list, app, Facebook page, Twitter feed or Instagram profile. There are endless delivery methods to choose from, but the goal is to be notified whenever there's a sale for your intended destination or from your airport of choice. It's important to find an alert system that allows you to act while sales and mistake fares are still available. Once a deal becomes common knowledge, hundreds of people start searching for the same flight and inevitably drive the prices up.

For those of you wondering what a mistake fare is, it's an error or miscalculation made by an airline that opens up tickets for a price that seems too good to be true, and sometimes is. A good alert program should let you know that a deal is a mistake fare, and inform you that there's a chance the airline won't honor the booking. If that occurs, you have the option of paying the difference in fare or getting a full refund, so you have nothing to lose by attempting to take advantage of mistake pricing.

My preferred flight alert system is Scott's Cheap Flights (www.scottscheapflights.com/). I first came across Scott

Keyes, the owner and founder of Scott's Cheap Flights, through Conde Nast Traveler. I noticed that Conde Nast's daily newsletter frequently featured headlines like "$400 flight to Paris" or some other enticing flight deal. Whenever I clicked on the link, the article cited to Scott as the person responsible for finding the deal. After seeing a few posts like this, I decided to cut out the middle man and go straight to the source.

Scott first entered the public eye when he received media attention for booking a flight from NYC to Milan for $130. Since then, he's published two books, built a million dollar business and grown his email list from 250 to 250,000 subscribers. His site offers both free and premium alert options, allowing you to get more emails and access "all the deals" if you pay to go premium. Here is an example of a premium deal:

WHEN: April through May 2018.

NORMAL PRICE: $900+

AIRLINE: American

BUY BY: We think these fares will last a day or two.

Some more great prices to Hong Kong!

No bag fees, etc.

All prices are for roundtrip flights and in USD unless otherwise stated.

TO:

Hong Kong (HKG)

FROM:

Atlanta (ATL) - $489
Minneapolis (MSP) - $489
Salt Lake City (SLC) - $489

HOW TO BOOK

Reminder: Scott's Cheap Flights does not receive referral fees from Google Flights, Momondo, or

The fee for premium membership varies depending on the type of payment plan you choose. The shortest commitment of 3 months costs less than $20 and pays for itself with your first flight deal. Premium members also get access bonus features, like the ability to filter deals by airport. You can cancel your membership at any time without penalty. If you're hesitant about paying, the free option is a great way to test the waters and determine if the list has any value for you.

THE DAILY TRAVELER

February 03, 2018

Fly to Greece for Under $500 Round-Trip

Hurry up and book—this deal won't last long.

THE DAILY TRAVELER

January 02, 2018

Fly to the French Caribbean for $178 Round-Trip

Trade the bitter cold for some much-needed Vitamin C.

In addition to Scott's Cheap Flights, there are several competitors that offer similar alert services. As I mentioned, Conde Nast Traveler's daily email newsletter (www.condenasttraveler.com/) is an interesting read and solid catch-all for sales. You may not see a flight deal in every headline, and it may not be an immediate notice since the newsletter is released daily as opposed to when the sale pops up, but I've seen deals in their emails for the first time. It's a good backup in case your alert system misses any airline not included in online search engines and is generally filled with useful travel content.

Travel Pirates (www.travelpirates.com/) is another competitor. They feature holiday packages and send alerts on cruises and hotels in addition to flights. Airfare Watchdog (www.airfarewatchdog.com/) boasts daily deals and notifies you when prices drop to a specific destination. The Hopper app (www.hopper.com/) notifies you of price drop as well. There are a few other sites I will list briefly in case they can be of use to you: The Flight Deal (www.theflightdeal.com/); Just Fly (www.justfly.com/); Holiday Pirates (www.holidaypirates.com/); The Fare Deal Alert (www.faredealalert.com/); Fly4free (www.fly4free.com/); Matt's Flights (www.mattsflights.com/). All of these sites aim to do the same thing—discover and share little-known travel deals.

Expats and international residents will want to check out Secret Flying (www.secretflying.com/). Their departure cities are typically outside the U.S. and they offer deals on hotels as well. It's worth mentioning that Scott's email alerts are expanding and incorporating more international departure cities. I've seen deals leaving from Canada, Australia and South America. Also, some of the alerts you see on websites are valid both ways, so if you find a fare from San Diego to Tokyo the deal could also work in reverse, from Tokyo to San Diego.

Alert sites all have social media accounts, allowing you to get notifications on your Twitter and Facebook feeds if you choose to follow them. I personally prefer the email delivery method because I know I'll see an email immediately versus risking that a social media algorithm will wait to show me a post 3 days later, but choose what works best for you. You might like the mobile apps because you get notifications straight to your phone. You might like websites because of ease of reading and RSS feed. Whatever your preference, pick a system that makes you feel like you're never missing out on a fare that's only available for a limited time.

A NOTE ON HIDDEN CITY TICKETING

I want to talk briefly about an app called Skiplagged (www.skiplagged.com/), which utilizes "hidden city ticketing" in finding deals. The premise behind this method is that airlines connect through cities that would be more expensive to reach outright. For instance, a flight to

Santiago, Chile might cost you $1500 to reach normally, but there's a deal to Buenos Aires, Argentina that connects through Santiago and only costs $350 (don't laugh, I've found a flight to Argentina at this price before!). The goal would be to book the second flight and abandon the plane when you get to Santiago, leaving the airport in Chile instead of boarding the connecting flight to Buenos Aires. This is a controversial ticketing method for several reasons.

Airlines actually penalize customers who use hidden city ticketing so you're advised not to use your account, airline credit card or frequent flyer number when making your reservation. Possible consequences include invalidation of airline miles and revocation of elite status. Guests who elect to use this method are unable to check a bag, as it would reach their final destination without them, so they're restricted to traveling with a carry-on only. Even then, travelers could run into trouble if their carry-on luggage gets checked at the gate.

Pro tip: Airline agents look for mini-suitcases to gate check. If you suspect this might be an issue on your upcoming flight, take a malleable bag like a backpack or duffel bag to minimize your chances of being selected.

Guests who utilize this method could delay a subsequent plane that's waiting for them to make the connection. They can also drive up fares for other flyers by creating a false demand. Finally, hidden city ticketing only works for one-way tickets, since airlines will automatically cancel any remaining flights on an existing itinerary once a connecting flight is missed.

Hidden city ticketing is looked down upon in the travel industry but is not technically illegal. You are free to use this method and I mention it because Skiplagged does feature amazing deals. If you decide to utilize hidden city ticketing, however, you do so at your own risk. Know that any of the flight alert systems I've already listed will provide you with similar results and none of the hassle.

1.2 Use a Flexible Search Engine

There are two different types of search engines: travel aggregators and online travel agencies. Travel aggregators, also known as a "meta search" sites, do not make your booking directly. They scan the web for the best prices and redirect you to the site of your choosing to book from there. They do not have booking agents standing by to assist you. Examples of popular travel aggregators are TripAdvisor and Kayak. In contrast, an online travel agency, or "OTA", makes your reservations directly and provides a customer service line to help with planning. Well-known OTAs include Expedia and Orbitz. For our purposes, we will label both sites collectively as "search engines."

Once you know there's a sale going on, you need to use a search engine to find and book your flight. Scott's email alerts typically include links to sample search results from two places: Google Flights (www.flights.google.com/) and Momondo (www.momondo.com/). Google Flights is my search engine of choice, for several reasons.

Google Flights has a map feature that allows you to see prices around the world from your departure airport of choice. You can narrow it down even further for specific dates. So let's say you know you have a week off in the summer, from June 1st to the 7th. You can put in your departure airport and chosen dates to see a world map with prices. You can then filter your results by prices and connections, i.e. only show nonstop fares under $500 roundtrip. This strategy is best for those who are open to different destinations and willing to follow the deal.

Another cool feature of Google Flights is the ability to search up to five different departure and arrival airports at once. This is useful if you know where you want to go already and need to compare prices to get there. You're only allowed to search airports within a certain distance of each other, usually a few hundred miles. So let's say I wanted to depart from Fort Myers. I could simultaneously search for departures from Miami, Fort Lauderdale, West Palm Beach, Orlando and Tampa to compare the best deals. Similarly, if I wanted to fly into Nice, France, I could compare fares arriving into Avignon, Monte Carlo, Lyon or Marseilles as well.

Remember that you don't have to arrive and depart from the same city. You can fly into Beijing, for instance, and depart from Hong Kong. It's possible to take yourself around a country, without a tour guide to set up your transport and schedule. It's easy to reach different cities via train or bus, and budget airlines in Europe and Asia make it so that flying is just as affordable and even more convenient.

Pro tip: Not every airline shows up on search engine results. Southwest Airlines and Allegiant Air require that you search for fares directly through their website. If you're flying within North America, it's a good idea to check these sites for comparison rates before booking.

For your reference, other popular search engines include the ITA Matrix (https://matrix.itasoftware.com/), CheapOAir (www.cheapoair.com/); Kiwi (www.kiwi.com/); Skyscanner (www.skyscanner.com/); Kayak (www.kayak.com/); Adioso (www.adioso.com/); Travelzoo (www.travelzoo.com/); Hipmunk (www.hipmunk.com/); CheapTickets (www.cheaptickets.com/); CheapAir (www.cheapair.com/), and; Seat Guru (www.seatguru.com/). Find the search engine that works best for you and always double check a few others on private browsing mode before booking just to be sure you're getting the best deal.

1.3 Best Booking Practices

ACT FAST

When you see a good deal, book it. Click the little red button that says "confirm." Don't wait till you verify that you have the vacation days at work or find a buddy who wants to go with you. By the time you finish pondering, the deal will be long gone and you never know when another one will come along.

Take comfort in the fact that most airlines offer a 24-hour refund policy, allowing you to cancel your purchase for a full refund within 24 hours of booking for *any* reason. The policy is actually mandatory for any flight involving a U.S. city thanks to the Department of Transportation, and it applies regardless of whether you purchased travel insurance. I'm a subscriber to the "book first, figure out the rest later" mentality, and taking that leap of faith has paid off in immeasurable ways.

BOOK YOUR VACATION PIECEMEAL

Those traveling on a budget will find success booking a vacation piecemeal. I look at planning vacations like a makeshift layaway plan. I commit to going on a trip for $1,000 total a few months down the road. To start, I might purchase my flight there for $200. Not only do one-way flights offer better redemption value for airline miles (to be discussed in depth in the next chapter), but it's often easier to pay one leg of a trip than both. A few weeks later, I'll book the return fare for about the same price.

Next I look at hotel bookings and apartment rentals. If the rental is cheaper, I pay for that outright (AirBnB requires full payment at the time of booking). If funds are low, I book a hotel with a "Book Now, Pay Later" option and make that payment the last "installment" of my pay-as-you-go vacation plan, for around $200-$300. I assess transportation options, booking trains or buses abroad, and a rental car if there is no public transportation available. I book activities sporadically throughout the planning process, either by paying online or resolving to pay upon arrival. Finally, I take out around $200-$300 in cash for my trip.

You can also book flight extras after your initial fare. Don't feel pressured to pay for baggage straight away or select your seat assignment at the time of booking. You can make these changes online after you pay, usually up to 4 hours before your flight. Wait to purchase extras until you know what you'll need.

AVOID PEAK SEASON TRAVEL

If you want to find a good deal, avoid peak season travel. This means any travel during the holiday season, specifically around Thanksgiving, Christmas and New Year's Eve. These are some of the highest traffic flight days, and airlines jack up their prices far in advance. If you know you have to travel during the holidays, your best bet is to book ahead of time since prices for the holidays rarely go down as the date approaches.

Another consideration is the temperature at your destination. Typically, summer visits or trips during dry season cost more than winter/rainy season tickets. This is because everyone wants to travel to the destination when the weather is nice, like July in The Netherlands or December in Australia. If you're willing to bundle up and carry an umbrella, you'll find off-season travel boasts fewer tourists at main attractions and cheaper lodging.

AVOID POPULAR TRAVEL TIMES

Generally, red eye flights are cheaper than flights during the day. You also want to aim for times that people do not want to be flying, like New Year's Eve or Christmas Day. This is a good strategy to minimize costs even during peak season. I've been in the air during the New Year's Eve countdown for the last two years, and saved hundreds of dollars in the process. Also, fly out on Thursdays instead of Fridays, and return on a Monday or Tuesday instead of

Sunday. You'll avoid the people who want to accommodate their work schedule and score better rates.

SEARCH INCOGNITO

Now more than ever, your online activity is being tracked. This explains why you google "hotels in Austin" one night, and suddenly ads for Texas hotels show up all over your Facebook feed. Conspiracy theories and novice shoppers alike will appreciate the suggestion to enter private browsing mode when searching for tickets. This prohibits the internet from tracking your activity and doesn't clue the airlines in to demand for your intended route. While you're at it, delete your browser history and cookies too.

There are mixed reviews over whether this is an effective strategy, with Skyscanner claiming that cookies from their searched won't affect your prices until you're redirected to the actual booking site, but in my opinion it's better to be safe than sorry. If there's a fare I'm worried will go up, I always switch to private browsing mode.

SEARCH FOR GROUP TICKETS INDIVIDUALLY

As a solo traveler I rarely search for more than one ticket, but those of you traveling with friends or family should search for tickets one at a time. Airlines may only have two tickets left at a set price, for example, and if you search for three you'll automatically be bumped up to the higher price bracket when you could have taken advantage of a sale. If you're worried about seat assignments, call the airline a few days before to see if they can assign you to the same row. You can also ask upon checking in, at the gate or, worse case scenario, ask someone to switch seats with you once you board.

ALWAYS DOUBLE CHECK

It's a good idea to double check one or two other online search engines before committing to a fare. You need to strike a balance with this tip, because you don't want your price to go up from too much searching, or the original deal to disappear because you waited too long. One option is to find the cheapest price on Google Flights. Then, once you know the date and flight information, search for the same ticket in Momondo on private browsing mode. Momondo is not as user friendly so it can be challenging to navigate if you don't know what you're looking for, but you can save $50 or more if you go there with a specific route in mind.

LET THE SALES COME TO YOU

Consider going where the sale is, even if it's not what you originally intended. I had no plans to visit Cuba in the near future, but when a $190 roundtrip fare popped up for Labor Day weekend, I couldn't resist. I gave the island a chance and had a great time. I drank my real mojito (anything you've been drinking before you arrive in Cuba is not a mojito—it's a mint leaf abomination), learned about recycled art from famous artists and cruised Old Havana in a pink convertible. It's a holiday I'll always remember.

1.4 What's a Good Deal?

So what's a good deal, and when should you book? You may have heard the myth that there are certain days that are better for booking than others, like Tuesdays. I haven't found this to be the case. Good deals can pop up at any time, and you need to be able to take advantage of them when they do.

Destinations that are always expensive to reach include but are not limited to: Japan, India, Kenya, Australia, Fiji, Antarctica, New Zealand, Russia and Abu Dhabi. If you find a deal for $500 or less to these places, you should take it. That's a steal, no questions asked. Also take the dates into consideration. It's hard to find cheap flights to Rome in July, or to a given country when they're hosting the World Cup. Peak season travel and special events means a seemingly inflated price can still be a good deal.

Other places are trickier. New York City, for instance, should never be costly to reach. Granted, you'll spend $100 just to get to and from the airport(s) since there's no effective means of public transport to any of the three in the area, but flying there shouldn't cost you an arm and a leg. With so many flights, you can get from New York City to anywhere in the world for a few hundred dollars roundtrip. Domestically, I've seen flights to NYC for under $100 roundtrip from cities like Charlotte, Miami and Dallas. If you've ever been to NYC you know you're sure to leave broke, but the cost of your flight shouldn't be the reason for that.

Like anything in life, finding good flight deals requires a combination of preparation and timing. I can't make airlines offer an error fare or host a one-day sale, but I can give you the means to be in the know when they do and tips to verify that you're getting the best deal. The rest is up to you.

CHAPTER TWO
An Introduction to Travel Hacking

"It's not the years honey, it's the mileage." –
Harrison Ford

2.1 Definition of Travel Hacking

The term "travel hacking" can be intimidating. It implies
that you're sitting in a room like Hugh Jackman in
Swordfish, maliciously tapping into airline databases in an
attempt to find a secret price. In reality, "travel hacking" is
a term used to describe everyday people using their miles,
bonus points or other rewards to get free flights and hotel
stays. For our purposes, we'll be limiting our discussion to
hacking flights.

Anyone who accrues frequent flyer miles, or points that can
be redeemed as miles, has the potential to become a flight
hacker. The moment they book a discounted award fare,
they are engaging in the act of travel hacking. First-time
redeemers might be surprised to learn that flights are rarely
awarded for "free." Even if your miles cover the price of
the airfare, there are still taxes and fees that are charged,
ranging from $5 to $100 or more depending on your
destination.

If you're serious about accruing miles and using them to
get free or cheap flights, the best place to start is with a
travel credit card. You do not need a travel credit card,
however, to be a travel hacker. The idea is to maximize

your non-cash purchases so that your groceries and electricity bill are helping to fund your future travels.

2.2 Travel Credit Cards

My first travel credit card was with JetBlue. I avoided credit cards for years, fearing I would get into debt and ruin my credit score. I had little to no credit, just a secured account I opened with Capital One and second subsequent account with the same bank, totaling less than $1,000 in an overall credit limit. When JetBlue approved me for a card, they approved me for $2,000. My credit utilization numbers were halved because my overall credit more than doubled. This made my credit score go up. When I applied for my second card, an American Express card with Delta, they gave me a $10,000 credit line. Using this strategy, I increased my credit score by more than 50 points in 6 months, simply by improving my debt to credit ratio.

I also got 5,000 bonus miles for signing up for the JetBlue credit card, after spending $1,000 in the first 3 months. Today, that offer has since doubled, up to 10,000 miles as a sign-up bonus for the JetBlue Card and 30,000 miles for the JetBlue Plus Card. This may not seem like a lot compared to other credit cards that offer anywhere from 50,000-100,000 miles upon sign-up, but JetBlue's redemption threshold is so low that with my 5,000 bonus points I was able to book a flight to Aruba for less than $70 roundtrip, booking piecemeal of course.

FORM OF PAYMENT	FARE TYPE	FARE	EXTRAS	$ YOUR PAYMENT	
				TAXES & FEES	TOTAL
Credit Card: M XXXXXXXXX	TBAWARD			USD15.60	USD15.60

FORM OF PAYMENT	FARE TYPE	FARE	EXTRAS	$ YOUR PAYMENT	
				TAXES & FEES	TOTAL
	TBAWARD			USD53.96	USD53.96

I share this with you to emphasize that anyone can use travel credit cards to their benefit. You do not need to be afraid of spending limits or worry that it'll ruin your credit. Quite the contrary, consumers are typically rewarded for playing the credit game, if they know how to play it wisely.

WHAT TO KNOW BEFORE APPLYING

Potential applicants should be careful with travel credit cards, for several reasons. First, they have an insanely high interest rate, usually between 20%-25%, so carrying a balance is not advisable. There's also a spending threshold associated with the bulk sign-up miles. Bulk sign-up miles are the biggest benefit to opening a travel credit card, so you need to make sure you'll meet the threshold and redirect all your spending onto the travel card at the beginning.

The spending threshold is usually anywhere from $1,000-$5,000. There are outliers, like the Citi Prestige Card that has a $7,500 spending threshold, but those cards come with benefits aimed to make up for the additional expense. Thankfully, you can use your credit card to pay for almost anything nowadays, including rent, bills and taxes. You can pay your mortgage with a credit card, though some services will charge you an additional fee. You can also prepay expenses ahead of time, like 6 months of your car insurance bill.

Be careful about closing travel credit cards. You may be tempted to cut your losses after you redeem the initial bonus miles to avoid the high interest rate and annual fee, but doing so could damage your credit since you're decreasing your overall credit limit and increasing your credit utilization rates. Also, several companies have a waiting period in which you can't re-apply for a card with them after you cancel, from 6 months to a year.

BENEFITS OF TRAVEL CREDIT CARDS

Now that we got the necessary warnings out of the way, let's talk about why you need a travel credit card in your life. Have you ever been pressured by the rental car attendant to buy additional insurance, sometimes costing more than the rental itself? A good travel credit card changes that, and provides insurance for any car rental paid in full with the card. Purchasing additional insurance at the counter will actually waive your right to coverage by the credit card company, so you can politely refuse the attendant and give an iron-clad excuse.

Another perk of travel credit cards is the lack of international transaction fees. I've paid with my debit card abroad before, and I still use it to withdraw funds from an ATM upon arrival, but I avoid using it overseas since I'm charged an extra $1 for every purchase I make. Instead, I rely on my travel credit cards while abroad since there are no transaction fees imposed on purchases.

DIFFERENCES BETWEEN TRAVEL CREDIT CARDS

There are three main types of travel credit cards: 1) co-branded credit cards; 2) credit cards that award travel credits, and; 3) credit cards that award transferable points. Co-branded airline credit cards are those affiliated with a specific airline. They offer perks aimed at frequent flyers, like free checked baggage, travel insurance and priority boarding. The JetBlue Barclay Card, the card I've been talking about, is an example of a co-branded card. They usually come with a bulk sign-up miles bonus and an introductory period during which they waive the annual fee. Afterwards, co-branded cards can include annual fees between $90-300.

Credits cards that award travel purchase credits, like the Capital One Venture Card and the Bank of America Travel Rewards Card, allow you to redeem your accrued points on anything related to travel, like rental cars or hotels. The Capital One Venture Card specifically offers unlimited 2x the miles on every dollar spent and 10x the miles for any hotel purchases made through their affiliate link. The benefit of these cards is that you're not tied to any one specific award program or brand.

Finally, there are credit cards that provide transferable points, like the Chase Sapphire Preferred card and the Premier Rewards Gold Card from American Express. These cards allow you to transfer accrued points to partner brands. This is a sort of middle ground, since you are limited to redeeming your miles with partner airlines and hotels, but you still have a dozen or more options to choose from.

TRACKING POINTS

You can track your points and rewards yourself on an excel spreadsheet, the old fashioned way, or you can sign up for a program that tracks them for you. The most common tracking programs are Award Wallet (www.awardwallet.com/), Loyalty Wallet (www.points.com/) and TripIt Pro (www.tripit.com/). TripIt Pro specifically requires a paid subscription and offers a host of other services. These programs will tally your miles, alert you when they're about to expire and track your trips.

You can also visit RewardExpert (www.rewardexpert.com/) to search for award flights from multiple airlines in one place. You can find the cheapest award route for your destination and track how many miles or points you've accrued towards the trip. Another paid program to help you find award flights is ExpertFlyer, (www.expertflyer.com/), which allows you to search more than 400 airlines for award space and upgrades.

It's worth noting that if you have a travel credit card, most will provide you with some sort of analysis and tracking on your dashboard when you log into your account, and send you alerts when you're close to a flight award to entice you to spend more.

WHICH TRAVEL CREDIT CARD SHOULD YOU GET?

The most common way of earning miles is through spending. Maximize your purchases to get double or triple points on things you would be buying or paying for anyway. Look for cards that offer these boosts on a regular basis, like the Capital One Venture Card.

If you have good credit and travel frequently, look into the Chase Sapphire Reserve Card. They have a $450 annual fee but you get a $300 annual travel credit and 3 times the points on travel and dining, as well as a credit to cover your Global Entry or TSA Precheck application. For most travelers, this is the Holy Grail of credit cards and has consistently been voted the number one travel credit card by consumers and travel insiders alike. At one point, they were offering up to 100,000 extra sign-up points for new card members, but that number has since been halved.

IN-FLIGHT SOLICITATIONS

Occasionally the offers that you get onboard an aircraft are worth considering. American airlines was recently offering 65,000 extra miles to anyone who applied for a card in-flight, 5,000 miles more than the individualized solicitations I was getting by mail. If you're not sure whether a particular offer is a good deal, wait until you've landed and do a quick Google search to compare bonus incentives. You can always hand the flight attendant your completed application on your way off the plane.

2.3. Earning Miles/Points

Aside from a bulk infusion of miles when you first open a travel credit card, there are several other ways you can accrue frequent flyer miles. Having a travel credit card will help you boost your earnings with these strategies but it's certainly not necessary. Here are some ways you can start earning and redeeming rewards today.

SHOPPING THROUGH PARTNER LINKS

Did you know that you could be earning miles for purchases you make at places like Amazon or Target? No credit card needed, just click the link on the airline's website to be redirected to the store's website and you'll automatically receive miles in your account for any purchases made. Some airlines offer two or three times the points per dollar spent, meaning that your $100 shopping spree on Amazon Prime could earn you anywhere from 100 to 300 frequent flyer miles, for items you were going to buy either way. Similarly, if you're booking a rental car, try to do so through an airline or travel credit card to get points for your purchase.

You need to be enrolled in an airline's frequent flyer program to take advantage of this method of purchasing. Also, you must buy through the link on the airline's website, otherwise they will not be able to track and reward your spending.

ADDITIONAL SIGN-UP BONUSES

Get points in bulk by signing up for an email list, rewards program or even following and engaging with a brand on social media. These are promotional offers that vary in compensation and duration. Look online for sites that aggregate and update these specials as they arise.

I found one site that lists the best deals monthly, at this address: www.hustlermoneyblog.com/complete-free-bonus-airline-miles-points-and-rewards/. There's also a website that allows you to search current award multipliers by your chosen store, brand or online market, found here: (www.evreward.com/).

COMPLETING ONLINE SURVEYS

This strategy takes a lot of time but can be effective if you're looking to kill time while watching TV at night. JetBlue offers 400 bonus miles for anyone who signs up for its online survey program, with 20-100 points awarded per completed survey and 10 points per failed survey just to compensate you for your time.

This means that even if you end up not being eligible to participate in the surveys, you're still accruing miles just by entering your details and answering a few multiple choice questions. This is one way to use your idle time to your benefit. E-Miles (www.emiles.com/) and E-Rewards (www.e-rewards.com/) are two survey websites specifically targeted towards traveler awards.

FREQUENT FLYER MILES

Make the most of your miles from flying. Sign up for all frequent flyer programs and make sure you're registering every flight you take since miles add up quickly. You can even get miles credited to your account from past flights if you have the details. You can also get awards from partner airlines. For instance, I was able to use my flight to Bangkok with Korean Air to accrue points on my Delta SkyMiles account since Delta is a partner airline.

When you have a travel credit card, the benefits are even greater. Most travel credit cards offer a mileage multiplier on flights purchased with your card, which is especially beneficial if you're traveling a long distance. You can also get points for purchases made in-flight, and buy snacks and drinks onboard at a discounted rate.

MANUFACTURED SPENDING

There are some people who take earning miles to a whole other level. A blogger friend clued me in to the concept of "manufactured spending," where you buy things that can easily be redeemed for money, like gift cards or money orders, in order to accrue points or miles. For instance, you could buy a $500 American express gift card, use it to pay off your credit card bill and you just earned 500 points without actually spending any money. You're usually charged a small fee to activate the card or proceed with the transaction, but at 1-2% it's a nominal charge that is worth the return on investment.

One extreme mileage user managed to skip having a car payment and utilizes a partnership with a rental car company to earn miles instead, boosting his renter status and drive a brand new car every day for less than the cost of a financed vehicle. Another manages to process $100,000/month in manufactured spending, bringing in nothing but rewards.

Done right, manufactured spending can be the Swordfish-inspired travel hacking of your dreams. It's the same tactics used by money launderers, so sometimes stores and banks will get suspicious and limit or stop transactions. One way to avoid this is to limit untraceable transactions, like Walmart Bill Pay. You may also be audited or monitored more closely. If you want to learn more about this advanced method of maximizing credit card rewards, this frequent flyer forum has loads of tips and is a great place to start: https://www.flyertalk.com/forum/manufactured-spending-719/.

A NOTE ON PURCHASING MILES

I do not recommend that you purchase airline miles. Sometimes you'll be prompted to buy miles in order to reach a threshold that you need for an award flight. Airlines also promote mile purchases by offering 20-30% bonuses. It may seem like a good deal at the time, but the cost of purchasing miles will often be more than the price of the flight itself. Any of aforementioned methods are more a cost-efficient way of boosting your overall miles tally without breaking the bank, and making sure you get something more out of it than just the miles themselves.

2.4 Redeeming Your Miles

Airline miles are the secret to reaching expensive destinations for next to nothing. Let's go back to the New Zealand example I cited in the beginning of the book. I signed up for a travel credit card that gave me 65,000 miles after I reached the minimum spending threshold of $3,000 within the first three months. Combined with 18,000 miles

I had previously accrued with that airline, I had a total of 83,000+ miles to spend. Believe it or not, these were not enough miles to redeem for a roundtrip flight to Auckland. I was disappointed, but persisted.

Using the fare finder calendar, I found the cheapest date for a one-way fare to Auckland instead. I also searched for a one-way return flight, but ultimately the fare there turned out to be the better value. For 40,000 miles and $38 in taxes and fees, I was able to secure a one-way flight to Auckland on a weekday. Unsurprisingly, the Friday and Saturday departures were as high as 90,000 miles each way.

Once I booked the flight there, I had to figure out how to return. I looked at the prices for neighboring airports and found a flight from Honolulu to Miami for only 25,000 points and $5.60 in taxes and fees. Hawaii is a domestic destination, so I assumed to be the main reason for the difference in redemption requirements. The final step was booking a one-way flight with Air New Zealand from Auckland to Honolulu, costing $285.97. My grand total was $329.27 for a roundtrip flight to New Zealand, including a 2-day stop in Hawaii.

The moral of the story? Don't get discouraged if the route you're looking for doesn't immediately pop up. There are ways to get creative and use your miles to get to your destination of choice, regardless of where that is.

HOW TO BOOK

The easiest way to book an award flight is to go directly to the airline's website and enter your search details, checking the box that indicates you want prices to be shown in miles versus dollars. Make sure to view your dates on a calendar so that you can identify the best rates. Flying on weekends, holidays or during special events can drive up the point values for an award. Most airlines allow you to view flights in different classes, so you can opt to redeem your miles for a first-class experience if you have enough available.

ONE-WAY FLIGHTS

A study from NerdWallet (www.nerdwallet.com/) revealed that consumers get better point values for one-way flights than roundtrip flights. There's also the added benefit that if something goes wrong, the remainder of your itinerary is not cancelled as it would be with linked a roundtrip ticket. Some airlines, like Delta, will offer you the ability to redeem your miles for a discount fare on roundtrip tickets only as an incentive to get you to purchase with them.

PURCHASES TO AVOID

Airlines might try to pressure you into wasting your miles by telling you they're going to expire or tempting you with catalogs of items you can get in exchange for your low balance. You should only redeem airline miles on flights, not magazine subscriptions or branded jackets. If you're worried the miles are going to expire, you have options to renew then, including transferring them, donating $1 to your charity of choice, making a credit card purchase or signing up for one of the survey programs outlined in the last chapter.

CHAPTER THREE
Flying on Budget Airlines

*"Feet, what do I need you for when I have
wings to fly?" – Frida Kahlo*

Have you ever heard of the cheap, fast and good rule? It
was originated to help navigate the food scene of New
York City. Basically, you can find food with 2 of the 3
traits, possibly less, never more. For instance, you can find
cheap food fast, but it won't be good. Or you can find good
food fast, but it won't be cheap. The same concept applies
to budget airlines. You can find a cheap route on a good
airline, but it won't be fast. Or you can find a fast route on
a good airline, but you'll be paying for the ride.

If you manage to find a flight with all three—nonstop, on a
5 star airline for a low price, jump on it. This is the unicorn
of all air fares.

Otherwise, it's important to accept that at times, you're
going to have to compromise. Those wanting to ensure they
find cheap flights may have to sacrifice on the airline
quality, time it takes to get to the destination, or both.
Thankfully, most budget airlines offer modern amenities at
an additional charge. We'll talk about what charges or
aren't worth paying for shortly. First, let's run through
some of the most popular carriers.

3.1 Common Carriers

There are over 100 budget airlines around the world, so I
won't be able to cover them all in this chapter. Instead, I'll

give you a rundown of some of the budget airlines I've previously flown with, and a brief review of my experience.

WOW AIR

I have to admit that I'm not the biggest fan of flying on Wow Air, but I love their insanely low prices so I keep coming back. I flew to Iceland nonstop for $99 with this airline, and came back for $239.99. Those were the exact prices, no additional fees or taxes added. I even had an entire row to myself on both flights, which almost never happens!

Still, it was a rough journey. There were no air vents on the planes so the ventilation was poor and it got hot and stifling at times. There was also no entertainment provided. I rented a tablet for an additional €25, but it was poorly equipped with a handful of little-known movie titles and TV episodes. If you do opt to fly with Wow Air, I recommend taking a red eye flight and trying to sleep through most of it. Otherwise, I suggest you download several Netflix series right to your phone so you have something to watch if you can't sleep.

RYANAIR

The best part about flying with Ryanair is that they're really, really cheap. I flew from Nice, France to London, England for a grand total of $23.20, and from Athens to Santorini, Greece for the same price! To put that in perspective, a ferry to Santorini sucks up 8 hours of valuable vacation time, whereas the flight is only 45 minutes and actually costs less! It's a no-brainer. Ryanair hosts sales regularly, so make sure you sign up for their email list.

If you have reserved a seat, Ryanair lets you check in up to 30 days before the flight. You'll want to queue up to board the plane as quickly as possible to ensure there's enough overhead bin space for your bag—it's a mad dash once boarding starts since people enter from the front and back of the plane and any bags that don't make fit are gate checked.

NORWEGIAN

I have to admit, after a few flights and a lot of comparison, Norwegian has grown on me. They are one of my favorite budget airlines for flying to Europe and have everyday low rates. At first, I resented that they charge for everything, from headphones to beverages, but now I just appreciate that they have these amenities available in the first place. They have a brand new fleet of planes, with windows that gradually tint as opposed to a cover that you pull down. There's a television on the back of every seat, and while you're given the option to pre-order meals there's also an *a la carte* menu that you can order from while in-board, with sandwiches and pizza and the like.

The biggest drawback when it comes to Norwegian is their carry-on policy. For Lowfare, Lowfare+ and even Premium tickets, the restriction is 10kg total for both your carry-on and personal item *combined*. That's only 22 pounds for both pieces. They are insanely strict on enforcing this policy and are the only airline I've seen with a scale at the gate. This means that it's nearly impossible to fly Norwegian without checking a bag. At least for me, my camera equipment alone is 5+ pounds, not to mention the weight of the roller bag alone. Keep this in mind if you're making reservations on multiple airlines since flying with Norwegian will likely require you to make a stop at baggage claim before continuing on to your connection.

SPIRIT

Many people hate Spirit with a passion. In fact, it's consistently voted the most hated airline in the U.S. They are notorious for delays and their planes are very basic. The seats don't recline, there's minimal leg room (28 inches) and the seat back tray table spans out maybe 6 inches. My biggest gripe with Spirit used to be that they didn't offer TSA Pre-check, so despite having paid for the service I always ended up having to make the longer security line. This changed in 2017.

Purchase Price	
Flight Price	$125.98
Base Fare	$125.98
Flight	$78.08
Unintended Consequences of DOT Regulations	$19.06
Passenger Usage Fee	$17.18
Government's Cut	$56.20
Security Fee	$11.20
US-International Departure Tax	$36.00
Passenger Facility Fee	$9.00
Total	**$182.18**

With expectations set so low, there's nowhere to go but up. That means that every time your Spirit flight is on time, or you have a comfortable trip, you're pleasantly surprised. Not to mention, if there's one thing they're consistent on, it's pricing. A roundtrip flight from Fort Lauderdale to San Juan only cost me $182.18, less than $100 each way. That was the standard price, without a sale, coupon or miles.

Just make sure to print your boarding pass out ahead of time. I can't tell you how many times I've taken a last minute detour to FedEx on my way to the airport because I refuse to pay the $10 fee for printing your boarding pass at the airport.

AIRASIA

I used this airline to fly in between cities in Thailand and Cambodia and had no complaints. Each flight cost less than $100 and included beverage service and a snack, regardless of its duration. There were a couple strange policies, like needing to turn off all electronic devices to watch the safety instructions (I haven't looked up for a flight attendant fastening a seat belt for years) and not being able to sit in designated premium seating, which exactly the same size and eerily vacant, but all in all this was a solid budget airline for traveling within Asia.

EASYJET

EasyJet is another option for flying within Europe. They're a no-frills airline but will get you from point A to point B for prices similar to RyanAir. They have an app that's easy to use and allows you to display your boarding pass. It's highly recommended that you download it prior to your flight as you're not able to print your ticket at the airport.

The airline lets you check in up to 30 days before your flight and reserve a seat at that time. Also, unlike Norwegian or other budget airlines, there is no weight limit on the bags you bring aboard. They're strict on size restrictions, so bring a malleable bag and you'll have an easier time passing the test.

SOUTHWEST

Southwest is a "love it or hate it" airline. As I mentioned, they don't show up on search engine results, so you have to book directly from their site. Their fares are rarely the lowest to a destination, despite their designation as a budget airline. You cannot choose a seat assignment. Rather, you have to check-in beginning 24 hours before your flight and boarding numbers and zones are then assigned on a first come, first serve basis. Once you're at the gate, you line up according to your zone and number and are free to sit wherever you like when you board. This means that the people in the later boarding groups get stuck sitting in the middle, and potentially splitting up their parties, without remedy.

I know people who set alarms on their phones to notify them exactly 24 hours before check-in. If you remember to do this, the system can work out in your favor. But if you're busy and forget, you pay the price for it. Not in fare, but in comfort and peace of mind when boarding. Sometimes, it's nice to be able to secure your place on a plane even if you come running up to the gate seconds before they close the boarding door.

ALLEGIANT

Allegiant Air is an American airline with low-cost routes within the United States. They are similar to Spirit in that they are very basic and don't have raving reviews. I've found that they're great for accessing smaller airports, and for domestic travel during the holidays. I was able to find a flight to Florida on the Sunday after Thanksgiving, typically one of the most costly flight days of the year, for just $132.

Receipt and Payment Details	
Airfare	$80.74
Fed Excise Tax	$6.06
Segment Fees	$4.10
PFC	$4.50
Sept 11 Security Fee	$5.60
Carry-on Bag	$18.00
Carrier Usage Charge	$13.00
Total Trip Cost:	$132.00

JETBLUE

I love JetBlue. They have the most legroom in coach, offering a whopping 32 inches per passenger. They have a television on the back of every seat, with free DirectTV and dozens of channels. They have excellent customer service and provide complimentary beverages and snacks. Not just pretzels either—I'm talking Cheez-It crackers, cookies and popcorn. Boarding is always a breeze and they never have any issues acknowledging my TSA PreCheck status. I could sing their praises all day long, but the reviews speak for themselves. JetBlue is the number one airline in America in terms of customer satisfactions, and they've expanded their routes to South America and the Caribbean. I cannot wait for them to start flying to Europe.

Another bonus of JetBlue is the ease of their award redemption. I touched upon this in the chapter on airline credit cards. Unlike other airlines, they do not inflate their mile redemption rates. They also frequently have sales with flights priced at $100 or less, requiring very few points for a reward flight. I was able to fly to Quito, Ecuador for $15.60 with JetBlue, and from Miami to San Francisco for $22 roundtrip. I'm consistently impressed by how far my miles go with them and will remain a frequent JetBlue flyer.

SWOOP

I haven't actually flown with this airline myself yet, but I mention it because they are well-known in Canada as the budget airline of choice and recently started promoting flights for $7. Their home page features flight deals within

Canada, under $100CAD, and they appear to be the equivalent of a Spirit Airlines or Allegiant for our friends in the North.

3.2 Avoiding Additional Fees

Budget airlines are notorious for added fees. After all, the cost is so low because it includes literally nothing. Some airlines have been known to charge for ice or water. While that's since been more strictly regulated, it's no secret that when you fly budget you get what you pay for.

If you're not careful, add-ons that allow you to fly in comfort can inflate the price of your ticket such that flying on a budget airline isn't even worth it. Let's run through some of the common fees associated with budget airlines and discuss what's worth the extra money, and what's not.

BAGGAGE

This is the easiest way to inflate the cost of a ticket. Some airlines, like Tap Air Portugal, charge €90 per bag, regardless of whether you purchase online or at the airport. Others, like Spirit, charge $100 per bag declared at the gate, regardless of size. What's more, the weight restrictions on carry-on luggage are so stringent that sometimes you're forced to check a bag.

Often, budget airlines have attendants double or triple checking your luggage for both size and weight before allowing you to board, and sometimes will make you gate check your bag before boarding, and pay for it. I've paid €35 to gate check a bag with Norwegian more than once, against my wishes. Assuming you're not connecting anywhere, that's still an extra €70 added to your fare.

Pro tip: If you purchase something at the Duty Free shop, no one will stop you from boarding with the easily identifiable duty-free bag. It can count as a makeshift third carry-on if you need somewhere to quickly stuff additional belongings.

SEAT ASSIGNMENT

How badly do you want that window seat? Badly enough to pay €35 for it, on each leg of your journey? This is a cost/benefit analysis you'll have to conduct on your own, depending on how long your flight is and how much the airline is charging for seats. The only way to avoid this charge is to let the airline assign a seat for you, which could very well lead to you being in the back row middle seat with a person reclined fully into your already limited space. Choose wisely.

BOARDING PASS

A lot of airlines, like EasyJet and AirAsia, have their own apps which allow you to get your boarding pass sent straight to your phone. Some airlines, like Spirit and Allegiant, will charge you to print a boarding pass when you arrive at the airport. Avoid these unnecessary charges and send boarding passes to your mobile if possible. Mobile boarding passes are also more likely to scan at the security checkpoint than printed tickets.

CREDIT CARD BOOKING FEES

Some airlines, like Ryanair, will charge you an additional fee for booking a flight with a credit card. This isn't just limited to budget providers and is a policy utilized by airlines like Qatar and Qantas as well. You can avoid these by paying with your debit card, paying with a gift card or booking through an American OTA, like Orbitz, since they're prohibited from assessing those additional charges.

FOOD AND DRINK

How do you feel about paying $12 for a ham and cheese sandwich, or $8 for a congealed microwaved pizza? That's what you're in for on most budget airlines. On Norwegian, you pay a whopping €45 to preorder dinner on your flight, and it's still airline food. It's not takeout from the Cheesecake Factory. Also, even though water is provided, it's not on demand and I've been on flights where they ran out of still water and only had sparkling water available. My advice is to stock up on your own food before you get to the airport. Buy the miniature Milano cookies or Goldfish Crackers at your local supermarket for a fraction of the price.

You can't bring liquids on board, but you can bring sandwiches, wraps, chips and candy bars. Think about the things you might buy at the airport or pack for a picnic. Don't bring anything that's prone to bruising or needs to be kept cold, like bananas or yogurt. Also, be considerate of your fellow passengers and avoid smelly foods.

Once you're past security, buy the largest bottle of water that will fit in your bag. I can't tell you how many times a liter of water has helped me through not only an international flight, but the first day at a new destination until I get my bearings. This is especially important if you're arriving at night and staying at an apartment or shared lodging instead of a hotel.

HEADPHONES

It's a minor cost compared to everything else I've listed, but it's a waste to pay €3 for headphones if you have at least 5 pairs lying around at home. Again, I'm looking at you Norwegian. Bring your own headphones to guarantee both savings and hygiene.

BLANKETS/PILLOWS

Some budget airlines will provide blankets and pillows for you on international flights, but others will charge a fee. A recent article in Conde Nast Traveler assessing the cleanliness of planes revealed that these extras get sanitized once a day on average, and are simply stuffed back in the plastic wrapping between flights. Again, save your money and avoid the germs by bringing your own. You can attach the pillow to the strap of your bag and lay the blanket on top of your handheld carry-on to save any valuable baggage space.

ALCOHOL

It used to be that getting free booze was one of the only perks of taking an international flight. On budget airlines, however, you pay for your drinks, alcohol included. This is where having an airline credit card for discounts comes in handy, so at the very least so you can take comfort in knowing your overpriced margarita is earning you 3x the points.

EXIT ROW SEATING

It used to be that meeting the minimum age requirement and being willing to assist in event of an evacuation was enough to merit you a place on the exit row of an aircraft. Today, it's considered a prime seat assignment with extra leg room, and guests are charged accordingly.

Airlines need to have the aisles large enough to accommodate foot traffic in the event of an evacuation, so these are the only rows in economy that they can't squeeze to the limit. You can't recline into an exit row, but you can recline if you're in the last row of the exit rows, so that's the seat to aim for. Unfortunately, airline providers are aware of the extra room and can make you pay as much as premium or comfort levels for the privilege.

BOOKING OVER THE PHONE

Since budget airlines want to minimize costs and employ as few people as possible, they often charge you if you need any kind of customer service or assistance. If you need to book over the phone or cancel directly with the airline, you could be charged a fee just for doing business this way. You are better off booking online.

3.3 Buying Direct from the Airline

I love using search engines to find great flight deals, but there are benefits to booking directly with an airline as opposed to third party vendors. When you book directly with an airline, there's a higher chance any mistake fare you find will be honored. Airlines are hesitant to invalidate a deal purchased directly on their website. Some airlines, like Lufthansa, will actually charge a fee for booking with third parties.

You also receive better customer service when you book directly with an airline provider. If you book with a third party, you may be redirected back to that site to handle any issues that arise. Third party websites could charge an additional cancellation fee on top of any airline charges. Airlines can see when you book with them directly, and agents are more willing to help you when that is the case than when you book through a third party site like CheapOAir.

Finally, some airlines will offer a price drop guarantee if you book on their website, issuing you a travel credit for the difference in fare if you find a better deal after your purchase. Alaska Airlines and Southwest offer this guarantee without any catch; they simply issue a travel voucher or airline miles to your account.

Other airlines like JetBlue, American, Hawaiian, Delta, United and U.S. Airways still offer a refund, with a few caveats. There must be a minimum fare difference, ranging from $75-$200 depending on the provider. There's also a fee associated with the refund, at times negating any would-be benefit. They also discourage you from making use of this policy by requiring you to call in to have it take effect versus being able to make the changes online.

They may not always be effective, but price drop refunds are a tool worth keeping in your cheap flight arsenal, and are more likely to work for those who book directly with an airline provider.

Pro tip: Apps like Yapta (www.yapta.com/), FairFly (www.fairfly.com/) and Flyr (www.flyrlabs.com/) will track your reservations after you make them and let you know if there is a subsequent price drop.

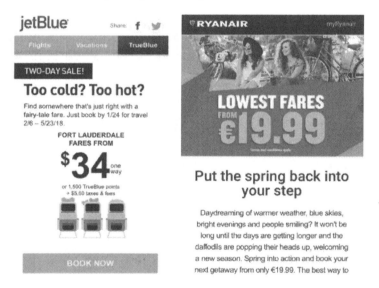

If you're going to book directly with an airline, your first step should be to sign up for their email list. This is the best way to stay in the know for all last-minute, wanna-get-away or even red-eye flight sales. You should be able to filter the deals by departing airport. As you can see from the first image above, JetBlue already knows Fort Lauderdale is my airport of choice since I have a frequent flyer account with them. These sales are for a limited time only, between 24-72 hours, and pop up once every 6-8 weeks. They will usually be for flights anywhere from 1 to 3 months out in order to sell vacant seats.

Another good way to buy straight from the source is to search the websites of your budget airline of choice. Wow Air and Norwegian are two of my favorites.

Wow Air has deals right on its homepage. They're arranged by the lowest price from an assortment of departure airports, usually $99 fares to Iceland. After that, they have fares between $149-$300 each way to destinations all over Europe.

I recommend that you view your dates in calendar mode to find the cheapest days to travel in a given month. As you can see, prices for the same route can range from less than $200 to $500 or more depending on when you fly.

							489.90
2	3	4	5	6	7		8
481.60	544.00	259.90	492.00		859.00	219.90	
9	10	11	12	13	14		15
405.00	499.00	189.90	375.90		454.00	189.90	
16	17	18	19	20	21		22
405.00	409.00	189.90	343.90		499.00	189.90	
23	24	25	26	27	28		29
260.00	369.70	189.90	343.90		499.00	189.90	
30							
352.50							

Return: Barcelona – Florida-Fort Lauderdale/Miami

April 2018

							426.50
2	3	4	5	6	7	8
	219.90		278.00		199.90	311.90
9	10	11	12	13	14	15
	199.90		278.00		199.90	328.80
16	17	18	19	20	21	22
	219.90		278.00		199.90	311.90

3.4 Pros and Cons of Budget Airlines

With so many choices for travel, and major airlines cutting back on what they offer passengers in an attempt to stay competitive with the rates, should you fly budget or steer clear? Here are some of the pros or cons for you to consider:

Pro: Cheap airline fares

The biggest pro of flying on a budget airline is that it's cheap. You can find great rates right on the homepage without coupons or thousands of airline miles. Anyone can start traveling today by hopping on a budget flight.

Con: Nothing included in your ticket

Those hoping to save with budget airlines have to be wary about added costs. Pack light and research the airline so your budget route doesn't come out more expensive than a regular, hassle-free flight.

Pro: Frequent promotions

Budget airlines are always running a sale. Just go to their website or sign up for email alerts to see what the best deals are from your departing airport.

Con: Restricted flight schedule

Budget airlines have a restricted timeline and only offer certain routes on certain dates. This means you may have no choice but to leave on a Thursday and come back earliest on a Tuesday, for example, because there are no flights back with that airline from Friday-Monday.

Pro: New planes

Since budget airlines are relative new, so are their planes. Some offer state-of-the-art features like automatic cabin light adjustments. They're just as safe, if not more so, than planes flown on non-budget fleets.

Con: Limited entertainment

The range of entertainment options could vary widely on budget airlines, from DirectTV with 70+ channels to no TV or even in-flight magazine. The chances of finding Wi-Fi onboard are slim to none.

Pro: Flexibility with planning

Budget airlines allow you to be spontaneous. As long as you have a passport valid for six months beyond your visit, you can travel at the drop of a hat thanks to low fares.

Con: Frequent delays

Unfortunately, budget airlines are notorious for being late. At the very least, you can take comfort in knowing that no airline is immune to delays, and that you didn't pay three times the money to be grounded during the same blizzard.

Pro tip: Under EU Regulation 261/2004, passengers are entitled to up to €600 in compensation for cancellations or delays of 3 hours or more.

CHAPTER FOUR
Other Money-Saving Strategies

"Many folks think they aren't good at earning money, when what they don't know is how to use it." – Frank A. Clark

4.1. Rule of Proximity and Flexibility

RULE OF PROXIMITY

Generally, the less jet fuel that a plane has to use to get to your destination, the cheaper your ticket will be. This means that it's in your benefit to choose a vacation destination in close proximity to you and your closest major international airport.

For instance, if you live in California, Washington or Oregon, you can access Canada, Hawaii and Asia for relatively cheap. It's much easier to find a Seattle to Japan deal than it is to find one from Atlanta.

If you live on the East Coast, like Pennsylvania, Virginia or New York, you can cross the pond to Europe. Those in Florida or Texas can easily access Central and South America. Anyone overseas in Asia can connect to neighboring countries on a budget. Similarly, Europe has dozens of countries that can be reached within the EU at under $100 roundtrip. You get my drift.

RULE OF FLEXIBILITY

Whenever possible, fly out of major international airports. The bigger the airport, the more flights there are, and the more likely that there will be open seats. Excessive open seats prompt the airlines to reduce fares in hopes of selling out the airplane, and that is why you'll see last minute sales and email solicitations.

I typically drive to Fort Lauderdale or Miami to catch a flight. It adds 2 hours to my overall commute, but the savings in airfare is significant. From Miami/Fort Lauderdale I have access to budget airlines and can find deals like a $200 flight to London.

In the same way your choice of departure airports could save you money, flying into a different arrival airport could reduce the price of your ticket. Take Morocco, for instance. Flying into Marrakech can be costly, but airlines like Tap Air Portugal frequently have $300 flights to Spain and Portugal. From either country, you can get to Africa for under $100 roundtrip, usually on a budget European airline like Ryan Air. This could be the difference between a $400 and $1,000 roundtrip flight to Africa.

The same strategy applies to domestic flights. I flew to Vegas for $200 roundtrip on JetBlue, nonstop. From there, I rented a car and was able to explore national parks in Utah and Arizona that would have been much more expensive to reach had I flown into Salt Lake City or Tucson directly.

4.2 Mixing and Matching Airlines

If the price is right, feel free to book your entire trip with the same airline. Otherwise, you'll likely have to mix and match providers in order to get the most bang for your buck. You can manage a seamless connection if you prepare for the realities associated with mixing and matching airlines ahead of time.

WHAT HAPPENS IF YOU MISS A FLIGHT?

If you have multiple flights on separate airlines and you miss one leg of your trip, the other airline is not obligated to rebook or reschedule you. You're not entitled to an automatic refund or guaranteed to be placed on standby for the next flight. Also, if you miss one leg of a roundtrip ticket, the airline you originally booked with will automatically cancel your return. I recently had the misfortune of missing a flight to Madrid, and my return flight was automatically cancelled despite pleas to the agents at the airport and multiple phone calls to their customer service line.

LEAVE TIME FOR YOUR CONNECTION

The most important part of booking flights on separate airlines is to leave adequate time for your connection, ideally 2 hours. If you're traveling internationally, you have to go through customs and security when you arrive at a new country, even if it's not your ultimate destination. You need to account for processing delays. Also, some airports are bigger than others, requiring you to take a shuttle or train transport to a different terminal for your connecting flight.

DON'T GET WEIGHED DOWN BY CHECKED BAGS

Another factor to consider when mixing and matching airlines is checked baggage. If your route is with separate air providers, you'll need to pick up your luggage at the carousel when you land at your connecting airport and re-check it with the second airline to your final destination. In some cases, you could be waiting an hour for your bag, and another hour to check in with an agent. This is why I always prefer to travel with a carry-on only. Just be careful yours doesn't look bulky or overstuffed, otherwise it'll be targeted for gate check once the cabin gets full.

VERIFY YOUR AIRPORT

Make sure that you're booking the same departure and arrival airport for your connections, especially when flying into a major city with more than one airport. I booked a connection to London Stansted not realizing my flight back to the United States departed from London Gatwick. It was a rookie mistake that could've left me stranded in the U.K., but thankfully I had an overnight layover and opportunity to adjust my plans accordingly.

4.3 Booking in a Foreign Currency

One reason travel hackers search for flights in private browsing mode is so airlines can't track where they're searching from. This is because airlines offer better deals to domestic customers than foreign visitors. For many, the thought of booking air travel in a foreign currency is intimidating. The truth is, this is a simple method of saving money on international flights. It may not save you hundreds of dollars like flight alerts or mistake fares, but it can save you anywhere from $50-$100 a ticket, and that adds up over time. All of this, and the only inconvenience you'll have to suffer is checking in for your flight in a foreign language.

To start, search for a good flight deal using the methods we've talked about. Once you find one, check to see if there's a local or national airline that's offering a comparable fare. Google Flights displays several different options, varying in duration and airline provider, ranked in the order of whichever route they think is the best value. You can also search Wikipedia to see all the airlines that service a particular airport. This is a great way to locate smaller airlines you may have never heard of.

Next, go to the local airline's website. Sometimes you can select your country of origin on the home page, other times you'll have to select a different country from the drop down menu. If you can't find the option to customize your language and country of origin, try searching for country code appendixes to site addresses instead. For instance, when you type ".es" instead of ".com" at the end of a website address, it will take you to the Spanish version of that website, if available. You can then search for the same flight, only in the country's local currency. If you're flying to Norway, look for flights in Norwegian krone. If you're flying to France, try booking in euros. You can play around with the fare conversions to see what country's rate is most favorable. Usually it's the country you're heading to, or the country in which the airline is based.

Make sure you check the terms and conditions before booking. It's rare, but some airlines have caught on to this strategy and make it so you can only pay for your flight with a card or bank account from that country. Remember to pay for your flight with a credit card that doesn't charge foreign transaction fees if possible to minimize additional costs.

4.4 Minimizing Airport Expenses

Airports are expensive if you don't know how to navigate them. Some costs are worthwhile, like the price of covering your checked bag in plastic wrap when you're going to Cuba, but others aren't, like the price of an airport taxi. With airlines trying to nickel and dime you every step of the way, you shouldn't feel bad about taking steps to limit additional fees.

TSA PRECHECK AND GLOBAL ENTRY

To get approved for TSA PreCheck and/or Global Entry, you need to submit an application, fingerprints, submit to a background search and pay the application. Some travel credit cards will cover the cost of applying for you. Without a doubt, both of these services are worth your investment if you're a frequent flyer.

If you don't travel internationally often, you can just apply for TSA PreCheck. When you're approved, you don't have to go through the normal security line. You can keep your shoes on and don't have to separate your electronics or liquids for the x-ray machine. You also sometimes go through a regular metal detector as opposed to the full-body scanner.

Pro tip: For expedited lines while traveling internationally without having to pay for Global Entry, download the Mobile Passport App. It's just as efficient as Global Entry and, better yet, free.

PARKING

I recommend that you avoid parking overnight at the airport. If you live near the airport, leave your car at home and take an Uber or Lyft to the airport. If you don't, check out Airport Parking Reservations (www.airportparkingreservations.com/). They show you places where you can park near the airport and have a reliable rating and feedback system. They also send out coupons routinely. Even if you don't receive one by email or see one readily available in the header of their site, you can do a quick Google search and Retail Me Not will usually have a coupon you can use to save $5 off your reservation.

This is one way to bring parking costs down significantly. For instance, at Fort Lauderdale Airport parking is $15/night, compared to $8/night at the off-site parking. For a week, that's a total of $105 versus $56, a savings of $49.

AIRPORT TAXIS

There are so many alternatives to airport taxis that these should be your last resort when you arrive at a destination. Your cheapest option is to take public transportation. Major airports like Amsterdam Schiphol and Paris Charles de Gaulle have trains that go straight to the airport terminal. Sometimes a public bus is also an option.

Your next cheapest options are to take an airport shuttle or shared riding service, like GoShuttle if you're in NYC, or call an Uber. If you do need a taxi, make sure you agree on the rate before you head to your accommodation. Taxis are a last resort but can be an affordable means of travel in places like Southeast Asia if you need a way to get around and are limited in options—my taxi from the airport to the hotel in Siem Reap, Cambodia was only $10.

EXCHANGING CURRENCY

The worst place to exchange money is at a currency exchange booth. You pay inflated exchange rates and higher transaction fees. Your best bet is to cut out the middle man and withdraw money directly from the ATM, in the currency that is used at your destination. Your banks will convert the charge at a more favorable rate and usually only charge $3-$5 per transaction instead of a percentage of the money you withdraw like an exchange booth might. Do not pick the option to withdraw your money from the ATM in dollars since it comes out cheaper if you elect to have charges made to your card made in the native currency. Avoid pushing "yes" automatically when asked if you want to pay in dollars.

Remember to let your bank know that you'll be traveling ahead of time, and ask about any withdrawal limits that may be in place. While you will undoubtedly find a lower ATM fee elsewhere, I recommend withdrawing money from the ATM at the airport upon arrival. It's unsure when and where you'll find a working ATM at your destination, especially in developing countries.

CHAPTER FIVE
Bonus Material

"It takes as much energy to wish as it does to plan." – Eleanor Roosevelt

5.1 25 Free Mobile Apps Every Traveler Should Have

Note: The more established a mobile app is, the more users contribute to its content and the more likely that content will be accurate. This is especially important when it comes to road closures or limited attraction hours. If you want an app you can count on, and download for free, big names are usually the way to go.

1) Google Translate

Language can be a formidable barrier when traveling internationally. So is finding free WiFi. Don't get caught in a sticky situation without a way to communicate. Download Google Translate, and save the language file you want to use to your phone before you go so you can use it anytime during your travels, no WiFi required.

2) WhatsApp

International data and texting plans are costly. Skip the fees and use WhatsApp, the preferred way of communicating overseas. I have contacts from India to Greece on my list. You can send text messages, call or FaceTime without worrying about an international data plan bill at the end of the month.

3) Mobile Passport

If you're still waiting in line after landing to get your customs pass, you're wasting your time. You can input all that information ahead of time into your cell phone, snap a selfie and head straight to the customs officer. This usually cuts your waiting time in half. If you subscribe to the notion that time is money, the Mobile Passport app is your new best friend.

4) Uber

Taxis are notoriously expensive, whether you're in New York City or Paris. While Uber isn't available everywhere yet, it's close and in more places than you'd expect, from Cairo to Cusco. Before leaving your hotel and hopping in a taxi, check the Uber fare instead and you may just save a few dollars while still boosting the local economy.

5) Grab

An alternative to Uber in Southeast Asia that allows you to book your driver right on your phone, track their arrival and pay by credit card. Currently, the app is available in 7 countries and riders can request a taxi, car or bike.

6) Waze

Wake keeps you in the know for everything road-trip related, from delays to police sightings. I've mainly used it in the continental United States. It relies on user data so you're likely to have more up to the minute updates in populated areas. This is also a solution if you're ever stuck in traffic generally and want to chat with drivers ahead about what's causing the problem.

7) TripAdvisor

There are countless trip planning tools and websites out there, but TripAdvisor is by far the most valuable. It has years of unfiltered customer reviews that you can search at the click of a button by keywords, instead of having to read through forums. Want to know if your hotel offers a hairdryer? TripAdvisor. Want to know if there's happy hour at the nearby restaurant? TripAdvisor. It's more thorough, updated and far-reaching than any other travel review website I've seen.

8) AirBnB

While not always your cheapest housing option, it's worth checking Airbnb to find apartments and alternatives to hotels. Beware of hidden fees at a given property, such as late check-in fees. Aim for a "Superhost," as the rating is periodically reviewed and has near perfect standards. Also, AirBnB has expanded now to include experiences, so this could be a good alternative to the Viator tours you usually book.

9) Capture

This is a must for GoPro users. You can preview shots on your device before taking them, use your phone as a remote through the app, and download all data directly from Capture. While video downloads take longer than photographs, all services are free and the app can be paired with your GoPro's WiFi so you can use it anytime, anywhere.

10) Overdrive

There's no such thing as too many entertainment options on a long-haul flight. Overdrive allows you to download books for free from your local library, straight to your phone or tablet.

11) LoungeBuddy

Airport lounges can be a great option for passing a long layover. This app lets you see lounges available in airports across the world, and tells you if you qualify for free or reduced entry because of a credit card, flight class, membership or elite status.

12) GasBuddy

This is similar to LoungeBuddy, only it lets you locate the cheapest gas stations near you. This is a must-have for any road trip. The only caveat is it's only available in America, Canada and Australia right now.

13) Rick Steves Audio Europe

The Rick Steves app is great for free audio tours of museums and walking tours of cities all over Europe. I always find the content thorough and entertaining, at times better than the paid audio guides museums offer. I only wish it wasn't limited to one continent.

14) Google Photos

Stop worrying about running out of space on your phone once and for all. Google Photos has virtually limitless space, backs up your photos automatically and can delete any photos it has already stored. The program will also edit your photos and movies for fun.

15) Google Maps

You can use Google Maps even while offline to access maps of the city you'll be visiting. Just log on to your account before you leave and download the content available for that area.

16) XE Currency

This app is also a website and allows you to convert money easily with live exchange rates.

17) Circa World Time

This app allows you to compare multiple time zones, allowing you to see what time it is in the U.S. before calling your family from Japan.

18) Hopper

Hopper will send you a notice when a fare for a specific route you inputted drops. You can then attempt to request a refund or credit.

19) Airfare Watchdog

This app monitors not just flights but hotel rates as well, so you can be sure you're getting the best prices on your trip.

20) Duolingo

Need to learn a new language quick? This acclaimed educational app promises to teach you languages like French or Korean with as little as 5 minutes a day.

21) SitOrSquat

This app will point you to the nearest public restroom and, as made clear by its title, will let you know what to expect once you get there.

22) CityMapper

With this app you can plan your route using public transportation. It features real-time departure information, details on delays and even walking directions to your nearest station.

23) WiFi Map

This app lets you see any available WiFi spots near you. The information is user generated and you're provided with a WiFi name and password for everything from public hotspots to hotel lobbies.

24) TodayTix

This is a must-have app for anyone visiting New York City. Avoid paying full price for Broadway tickets and chose from empty seats the week of our visit instead, for a fraction of the price.

25) HostelWorld

If you want to stay at a hostel, this is the best booking site to see all your options in one place.

Pro tip: Stop paying for guidebooks. Your local library has a travel section filled with the same books for free. Most libraries include a 3-week rental, not counting renewals, so if the book is compact you can bring it along with you. They come with the same maps and handouts. Not to mention, libraries periodically review and renew their collections, especially with travel content, so you'll likely have the newest edition.

5.2 Best Websites for Living and Working Abroad

For some of you, it's not enough to just fly to destinations on a frequent basis. If you aspire to live or work abroad, you may be unsure where to begin. If you're just starting out as an expat or want to find ways to get creative with food and lodging while traveling long-term, check out these 9 alternative travel websites.

1) Workaway (www.workaway.info/)

Workaway is an international service that allows users to arrange homestays and cultural exchanges. Guests help out on various tasks in exchange for free lodging and food. Visits can last anywhere from a few days to a few months, depending on the arrangement. You create a profile on their website, specify the country you want to go to and the type of work you want to do. Then you can search for hosts and reach out to them directly if the opportunity seems appealing.

You have to pay to establish an account and gain access to Workaway's database. Currently, the cost is $34 per person per year or $44 per couple if you're traveling with a friend or significant other.

2) Help Exchange (www.helpx.com/)

HelpX is an online listing of farms, homestays, ranches, lodges, B&Bs, hostels and even boats who invite volunteers to stay with them short-term in exchange for food and accommodation. There are two types of membership: free and premium. With the free membership, you create a profile and hosts reach out to you. The premium membership allows you to search their database, contact the hosts, view past reviews and list location and work preferences. The cost is €20 and membership lasts for two years.

3) Hippohelp (www.hippohelp.com/)

Unlike HelpX and Workaway, Hippohelp is a completely free service. Volunteers have the option of signing up through their Facebook account instead of the website. You can also browse the available listings without creating a profile first. It has a map-based interface so you can easily scout for opportunities in your area.

4) WWOOF (www.wwoof.com/)

Worldwide Opportunities on Organic Farms, or "WWOOF" for short, is an organization limited to facilitating stays on farms. This is great for those with an interest in sustainable travel or horticulture. Unlike the other sites, there is no international membership. WWOOF organizations and entry fees vary by country, and you have to check each country's WWOOF page separately for details.

5) Volunteers Base (www.volunteersbase.com/)

Volunteers Base markets itself as the completely free alternative to the volunteer and work exchange websites listed above.

6) TrustedHousesitters (www.trustedhousesitters.com/)

This is the most recognizable name in the housesitting game, but you have to pay to play. It costs $119/year to have access to the website and its listings. They boast a pretty website design and robust affiliate system. Generally, housesitting assignments require you to also take care of things around the property, like watching a pet or plants.

7) MindMyHouse (www.mindmyhouse.com/)

This is another housesitting site. It's not as pretty and has less listings but also has less users and a better opportunity to climb to the top of the member rankings for potential assignments. Another perk of this site is the low annual fee, just $20.

8) HouseCarers (www.housecarers.com/)

Running since 2000, HouseCarers is one of the oldest and most established housesitting sites. Membership costs $50 a year and listings are primarily available within the United States.

9) Nomador (www.nomador.com/)

Nomador is the only housesitting site that offers users a free membership option, so it's ideal for part-time sitters and travelers. You get fewer features with the free option. Premium membership costs $89/year or $35/quarter. The site is heavy on European sits and has a blind two-way review system like AirBnB.

10) Jooble (www.housecarers.com/)

With placements in over 60 countries, Jooble is a great place to start your international job hunt. It's especially helpful for finding work in developing countries.

11) Go Abroad (www.goabroad.com/)

Go Abroad allows you to teach, volunteer or intern abroad. It's geared more towards students and new graduates and they try to help applicants find scholarships to help cover the cost of airfare.

12) TEFL Online (www.tefljobplacement.com/)

This site offers an online certification program to allow you to teach English internationally. It also has a job board where you can search for teaching opportunities, primarily in Asia.

5.3 20 Side Hustle Ideas to Boost Your Travel Funds

We could all use a little extra money to travel. To fund my year of adventure, I taught English online with VIPKid. You may be contemplating getting a side hustle, but are scared to invest your time and money into something that might not pan out. You could also be worried about whether or not you can manage the additional demand on your already limited time.

The good news is, you don't need a lot of money to get started, and side hustles are flexible by their very nature. They should easily fit into your schedule and take up only as much time as you want to devote to them. If you need ideas to help you get your side hustle on, here are 20 ideas to help you start earning money today.

1) Teaching

As I mentioned, I teach English online. The company I work for requires a degree and American accent, but there are many competitors. You're also not limited to teaching English, you can teach any language or subject. If tutoring online sounds up your alley, check out WizAnt and Skooli. You can also look into test prep specifically if you've gotten a high grade on a qualifying exam like the MCAT or LSAT but don't necessarily have teaching experience.

2) Start an Etsy shop

Are you artsy? Can you sketch/draw/paint? Sell your pieces. Can you scrapbook? Do you make cute jewelry?

Soap? Wreaths? List them for sale on Etsy. Love making gifts for your kids? There's a site dedicated to letters from Santa. You could do something similar, like letters from a Disney Princess.

3) Sewing

Alterations are in high demand nowadays. Offer your services online or through a local dry cleaner. Post flyers at a gym where people might lose weight or need clothes taken in. Capitalize off fraternities and sororities on college campuses that always need letters sewn onto their shirts and memorabilia—you can charge anywhere from $30-$100 per piece depending on the type of article of clothing, all for sewing on three Greek letters.

4) Virtual assistant

Bloggers are busy and constantly looking for assistants to help with tasks like creating Pinterest pins and Facebook posts. If you're social media savvy and have knowledge of basic programs like Canva, Wordpress and Hootsuite, then this is a great way to make extra cash entirely online.

5) Freelance writer

You can make money as a freelance writer by pitching to different websites. PennyHoarder, Upworthy and Saveur are examples of well-known sites that pay their writers.

6) Utilize your car

If you have a car, spotless driving record and don't mind driving others around, check out ride-sharing services like

Uber and Lyft. If you want to deliver purchases instead, look at Postdates and Uber Eats. Finally, if you don't mind renting out your car and prefer a hands-off approach, look at Turo, a peer-to-peer service where people pay you to use your car for a period of time.

7) Run errands

You can become a tasker on TaskRabbit to you cash in on everyday errands, like furniture assembly, home repairs or moving and packing services.

8) Proofreader

Do you have an eye for details? You can do proofreading for individuals or on contract with companies.

9) Tax prep

Tax season sees the biggest boost in temporary employment. Even if your knowledge of tax preparation is limited to inputting numbers from a W2 form into the TurboTax software, you could charge for simple returns.

10) Rent out your space

You can rent out an extra room in your house on AirBnB. If you're not comfortable renting out your living space, try the Garage app instead, an app that lets you rent out your parking space or driveway when you're not using it. This is great if you live near college campuses or sports arenas.

11) Sell produce

Do you have a green thumb? Sell herbs, flowers, fruits or vegetables at your local farmer's market.

12) Hair/makeup

Are you good at cutting and styling hair? Offer bridal parties services at discounted rates to get you started, and ask for referrals. Create YouTube tutorials to build a following and establish credibility.

13) Baking

Can you bake well? Cake decorating for birthday parties or showers is great if you have the skill set for it. You can also pick a specialty and offer treats only around holidays, like cookie bins, cupcakes and cake lollipops.

14) Sell your photos

If you take good photos, consider selling them on sites like iStockPhoto, Shutterstock and Getty Images. If you have the equipment and an entrepreneurial spirit, you could start your own photography company. You can specialize in any number of areas like boudoir, professional portraits, real estate sales, landscape or even seasonal shoots. Bonus points if you have a drone.

15) Music lessons

If you can play an instrument, you can make good money teaching others at your leisure. Try to tutor privately or apply to give lessons at a local music school.

16) Become a tour guide

Do you know your neighborhood? If you know the best spots to eat, consider guiding a food tour. If you're a nature fan, consider leading hiking or kayaking tours. Love art? Try giving a walking tour of the city's best street art or museums.

17) Freelance designing

Do you have art skills and basic knowledge of Adobe Photoshop? What about a working knowledge of Canva and the ability to make Facebook covers and optimized pins? If you can design, you can sell your work on places like 99 Designs and Fiverr.

18) Adjunct professor

Do you have a professional skill? Maybe you're an accountant who's good at business bookkeeping, or a nurse who's excellent at doing PICC lines. Consider becoming an adjunct professor for a nearby college or community school.

19) Refurbish and resell

If you have an eye for diamonds in the rough and are able to refurbish furniture, try finding cheap pieces on Craigslist and bringing them back to life. A vintage chair may cost you $15 on the site, $100 for materials to repair and sell for $300 depending on its age and quality of the craftsmanship.

20) Get certified

You can get a notary certification or become a loan signing agent certified to oversee mortgage signings. You can also get ordained online and perform marriage ceremonies.

About the Author

Jen Ruiz is a solo female travel blogger and lawyer who has been featured by The Washington Post and ABC News for her budget travel secrets. She is also a freelance travel writer with bylines in Matador Network, Paste Magazine, Elite Daily and BlogHer, among others.

In 2017, Jen set out to take 12 trips in 12 months while employed full-time as an attorney for a nonprofit organization. She surpassed her goal, completing 20 trips in 12 months to destinations like Greece, Iceland, Cuba, France, Puerto Rico, Italy, France and Cambodia. She went on the majority of these trips on her own and doesn't believe in waiting for the perfect circumstances to start seeing the world.

Jen chronicles her adventures and shares travel advice on her website, www.jenonajetplane.com/. She is currently working on her next book and hopes to inspire young professionals to live life beyond the constraints of their 9-5 jobs and student loan obligations.

Jen is active on Facebook, Twitter, Instagram and Pinterest, feel free to reach out and follow along! Also, if you found this book helpful, please leave a review on Amazon. Your support will help spread the word and allow others to take advantage of affordable flight deals.

Made in the USA
San Bernardino, CA
11 June 2018